The People's His

County Durham And Northumberland During The Second World War

by

Geoffrey Berriman

I dedicate this book firstly to my sister, Joan, who was a schoolgirl in Chester-le-Street, Co Durham, during these difficult times, and who having personally encountered the stark realities of war has led her life with determination and so successfully.

I also dedicate it to all the people of Northumberland and Co Durham who played their part, whether in a civilian or military role, either at home or overseas.

Copyright Geoffrey Berriman 2005

First published in 2005 by

The People's History Ltd
Suite 1, Byron House
Seaham Grange Business Park
Seaham
County Durham
SR7 0PY

ISBN: 1 902527 17 8

Contents

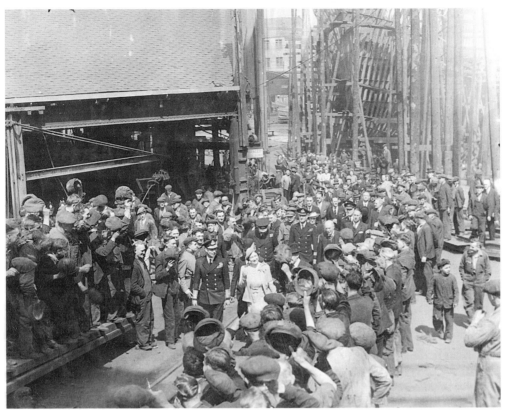

The King and Queen visit the Doxford Shipyard, Sunderland on 7th April 1943.

Introduction

In compiling this book I have tried to include as many aspects as possible of life in Co. Durham and Northumberland during 1939 to 1945. I have also devoted a substantial part to people from the two counties, who, as a result of the war, found themselves serving in other parts of the country or the world. Where I have not included photographs of some aspects of wartime life or of particular fighting units connected with the counties, this has often been due to the difficulty in finding suitable pictures despite making extensive enquiries.

I hope that one result of the book might be that if there are readers who do have photographs taken during the wartime period, they will one day consider passing these on to a Museum, one of the County Archives/Records Offices, a Library, or to a Military Archive like the Second World War Experience Centre at Horsforth, Leeds, where they will be available for research in the years to come.

Geoffrey Berriman
Witton Gilbert, Durham
October 2005

Abbreviations

Many readers will be familiar with the abbreviations given in the book and they will require no explanation. However, for those who might need some assistance, I have often given the meanings. I also give in the table below the meanings of some of the more commonly used abbreviations.

AFS	Auxiliary Fire Service
ARP	Air Raid Precautions
ATS	Auxiliary Territorial Service
CBE	Commander of the Order of the British Empire
DFC	Distinguished Flying Cross
DLI	Durham Light Infantry
DSO	Distinguished Service Order
MC	Military Cross
MM	Military Medal
MTB	Motor Torpedo Boat
OBE	Officer of the Order of the British Empire.
POW	Prisoner of War
RAFVR	Royal Air Force Volunteer Reserve
RNF	Royal Northumberland Fusiliers
RNVR	Royal Naval Volunteer Reserve
VE	Victory in Europe
VJ	Victory in Japan
VRD	Volunteer Reserve Decoration
WVS	Women's Voluntary Service

Acknowledgements

I wish to thank the following who have provided me with so much useful information, and in many cases photographs from their own collections: Mrs. Shirley Annand MBE, Mr Les Bell, the Collection of the late V. Blankenburgs in the Northumberland County Archives Service, Mr John Brereton, Mrs Pam Campbell, Mr George Dickinson, Mr Jack Geddes, Mr and Mrs Trevor Glen, Mr Denis Gowans, Mrs Shirley Harrison, Mr David Kayll, Mr John Lawlan, Mr Bill Leadbeater, Dr Joan Lodge, Mr John Metcalfe, Mr George Nairn, Mrs Carol Oliver, Miss Brenda Reay, Mr Arthur Rodgers, Mr S. Rutherford, Mr David Souter VRD, Mr and Mrs David Storey, Herr Otto Taufratshofer, Mrs Lorraine Thompson.

A great deal of assistance has been given to me by Archives and Record Offices, Museums and Libraries in providing photographs and information and I am pleased to acknowledge their help. Where I have dealt mainly with particular members of staff I have placed their names in brackets after the names of the institution, though all other staff I have met have also always been very helpful: Beamish Photographic Archive (Mr Julian Harrop and Ms Carolyn Ware), Bishop Auckland Town Hall, Centre for Local Studies at Darlington Library (Mrs Lynne Litchfield, Mrs Kimberley Bennett and Mrs Katherine Williamson), Durham County Council (Mrs Anita Thompson), Durham County Records Office (Miss J. Gill, Mrs Liz Bregazzi and Mrs A. Jackson), the Borough Council of Gateshead (Mrs Anthea Lang), Hartlepool Arts and Museum Service (Miss Charlotte Taylor), Hartlepool Borough Libraries (Mrs Maureen Dickinson), the Imperial War Museum (Ms Yvonne Oliver and Ms Sarah Martin), the Ministry of Defence (Miss Roberta Twinn), Newcastle Libraries and Information Service (Mrs Olive Graham and Mrs Sylvia Walker), Northumberland Records Office (Mrs C. Scott), North Tyneside Metropolitan Borough Council (Mr Alan Hildrew), The Royal Northumberland Fusiliers Museum (Mrs Lesley Frater and Mrs Gemma Bates), South Tyneside Metropolitan Borough Council (Mr K. Bardwell), Stockton Borough County Library Services (Ms Barbara Baker), Sunderland City Council (Mr Phil Hall and Miss Jane Hall), Tyne & Wear Museums (Mr Gary Woods, Mr James Fell and Mr Martin Routledge), Tyne & Wear Archives Service (Ms Liz Rees).

I should like to thank Mr Andrew Clark of The People's History, who has, as always, been so very supportive during the compilation of this book.

The two photographs on page 117 are reproduced by kind permission of Mr. Rolf-Werner Wentz.

SECTION ONE

PREPARATIONS FOR WAR

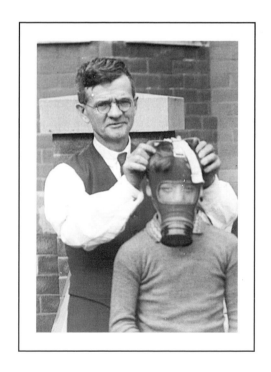

Prior to the declaration of war on Germany on 3rd September 1939, the possibility of war had been anticipated for some time. In 1938 air raid trenches were dug in public parks. Reservists were called up for military service, and civilians were issued with gas masks. A declaration between Great Britain and Germany ended the crisis, and many felt that war had been averted. Early in 1939, however, it became clear that Hitler was intent on gaining territory in Europe, and that war was likely after all. As September approached, reservists were again called up, air raid shelters were built, and plans made to evacuate children from urban areas to safer rural areas.

Air raid shelters being built at the Market Place, South Shields, 1939.

Entrance to Victoria Tunnel in the grounds of St Thomas' Church, Newcastle. Completed in 1842, the tunnel was used as an Air Raid Shelter during the Second World War and could take 9,000 people.

An Air Raid Precautions exercise outside the Newcastle Golf Club building in Claremont Road, Newcastle, February 1939.

ARP trench lining in Newcastle, February 1939.

Air raid shelters at Ouseburn Culvert, Newcastle.

Air raid shelters at Joicey Square, Stanley, Co Durham, 1939.

Above: ARP Drill at North Road
Works, Darlington.

Right: An advert for the building of
air raid shelters, September 1939.

A Decontamination Squad scrubbing a road during an exercise in Newcastle in 1939 as part of the procedure for dealing with Mustard Gas which it was thought the Germans might use against the civilian population. In fact this gas was never used.

An early wartime photograph of First Aid Nurses at Chester-le-Street.

City and County of ![crest] Newcastle upon Tyne.

Evacuation of School Children and certain other Persons
in the event of a War Emergency.

1. It is necessary that the contents of this notice should be known to EVERY CITIZEN OF NEWCASTLE UPON TYNE.

2. Do not be alarmed because this notice has been sent to you. We do not claim to have any more information than you regarding the international situation ; we do not know whether the arrangements to secure the removal of the children and other persons needing special care to a less crowded place will ever be used ; we earnestly hope that they will not ; but for the sake of the children and of the others needing special care we must all be prepared. Better arrangements can be made in the calmness of peace than in the anxiety of war.

3. It is not an easy job for the teachers and officials of the City, the railway companies, the traffic commissioner and the bus companies to arrange for over forty thousand school children to be removed in a single day to less crowded districts where they may be housed, fed and educated. and for about the same number of other persons needing special care to follow them the next day. It is very public-spirited of the officials, teachers and other friends in the less crowded areas to make billeting and educational arrangements for the benefit of our citizens and children, and of householders in those areas to receive our dear ones into their homes.

4. Before the time fixed for the return of the forms enclosed, meetings of parents will be held in the schools, when fuller information will be given and questions may be asked.

5. If you still find it hard to understand anything in this notice, talk it over with your wife (husband) and friends or call at the nearest school where the head teacher will gladly welcome you and will be ready as always, to do all he (she) can to help you.

6. So we ask you to give us the information we seek. By doing so quickly and carefully you will be helping yourself, your families and your friends, as well as those whose public duty it is to undertake urgently a task of great magnitude and difficulty.

WILLIAM R. WALLACE, Lord Mayor.

GEORGE DIXON, Sheriff.

JOHN ATKINSON, Town Clerk and Evacuation Officer.

THOMAS WALLING, Director of Education and
Schools' Evacuation Officer.

The first page of City and County of Newcastle notice to every citizen about evacuation of schoolchildren and others.

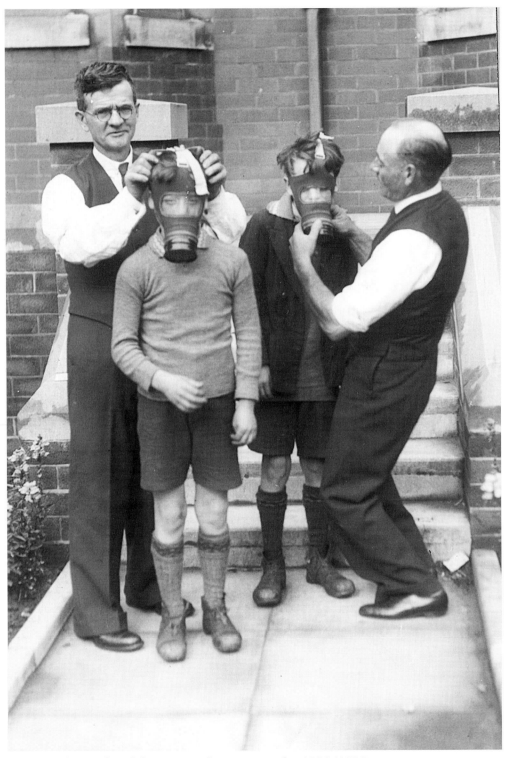

Children being fitted for gas masks, Newcastle, 1938/1939.

Above: Gateshead schoolchildren leaving for evacuation 1939. They are carrying their gas masks in boxes.

Right: Thousands of children were evacuated to country areas from urban areas, which were vulnerable to bombing. Some went overseas to Canada or America. The photograph shows Gateshead children leaving for evacuation in 1939.

A group of evacuees from Gateshead and Tynemouth on 8th September 1939, possibly in Co Durham or North Yorkshire.

Evacuees and their mothers from Hartlepool, Co Durham, at Scarborough.

AIR RAIDS

The industrial and coastal areas of the counties suffered heavily from air raids, and there were numerous civilian casualties in Newcastle, North Shields, South Shields, Tynemouth, Sunderland and Hartlepool. Country areas were not unaffected as they too were subjected to bombing when fatalities sometimes occurred.

Air raid practice at the Blue Coat School, Durham, on 3rd November 1939.

Wearmouth Drive, Sunderland, following a raid on 15th August 1940 when the Battle of Britain was at its height.

Faulder Road, West Hartlepool, after an air raid on 25th/26th August 1940.

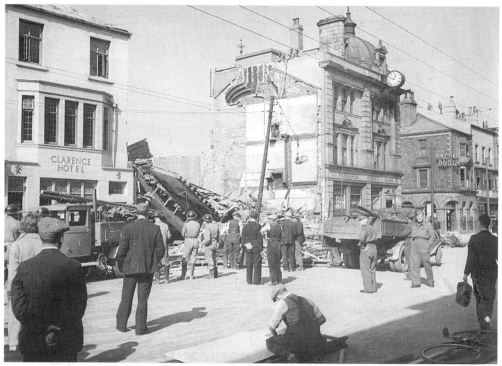

Church Street, West Hartlepool, after an air raid on 26th/27th August 1940 when three people were killed.

Biddlestone Crescent, North Shields, after an air raid on 9th/10th April 1941 when thirty-five people were killed and one hundred and five were injured in the Tynemouth area.

Brandling Terrace, North Shields, after the air raid on 9th/10th April 1941.

Fawcett Street, Sunderland, following an air raid on 9th/10th April 1941.

Air raid damage at Forth Banks, Newcastle. There were heavy raids over Newcastle in 1941. Forty-seven people were killed in a raid on 25th April and fifty in a raid on 1st September.

Ocean View, Whitley Bay, following the dropping of two land mines on 16th April 1941.

Brenda Road, Hartlepool after an air raid.

Bomb damage at George Street/King Street, North Shields, which occurred in a raid on 3rd/4th May 1941. One hundred and five people were killed in North Shields in this raid, the worst bombing incident on Tyneside during the war.

About fifty German bombers raided South Shields on 2nd October 1941. Twelve people were killed, and a great deal of damage occurred. The photograph shows Market Place after the raid.

Marlborough Street, South Shields after the raid on 2nd October 1941.

A view of bombed housing at St George's Road, Cullercoats, probably after the raid on 11th/12th October 1942 when six people were killed.

Howick Road, Sunderland, after a raid on the town on 15th/ 16th May 1943 when seventy people were killed and eighty-two seriously injured.

Cauldwell Villas, South Shields, after an air raid on 12th March 1943.

St Michael's Church (now Sunderland Minster), the Empire Theatre and the Almshouses following an air raid over Sunderland on 24th May 1943, which was the last major air raid on the North East. Eighty-three people were killed and two hundred and twenty-two were injured in the town during this raid.

Bomb disposal squad dealing with an unexploded bomb at the corner of Farnham Terrace and Chester Road, Sunderland, on 16th May 1943.

An Army salvage unit in Durham, 1941. Army salvage units followed the bomb disposal squads and cut up unexploded bombs.

PERCY CRESCENT & COCKBURN TERRACE FIREWATCHING ROSTER.
FROM 22ND MARCH, 1943.

Mr. S. Tait, Mr. J. Waterworth.	Mar 22	Apl 3	Apl 15	Apl 27	May 9	May 21	Jun 2	Jun 14	Jun 26	Jul 8	Jul 20
Mr. A. Stapley. Mr. A. Tait.	23	4	16	28	10	22	3	15	27	9	21
Mr. J. Foster. Mr. T. Corcoran.	24	5	17	29	11	23	4	16	28	10	22
Mrs. Dagg. Mr. E. Roberts.	25	6	18	30	12	24	5	17	29	11	23
Mr. Henderson. Miss Henderson.	26	7	19	May 1	13	25	6	18	30	12	24
Mr. Osborne. Mr. Barrow.	27	8	20	2	14	26	7	19 Jul 1	1	13	25
Mr. Couchman. Mrs. Couchman.	28	9	21	3	15	27	8	20	2	14	26
Mr. J. Dugdale. Mr. W. Dugdale.	29	10	22	4	16	28	9	21	3	15	27
Mr. W. Brown, Jnr. Mr. Stapylton.	30	11	23	5	17	29	10	22	4	16	28
Mr. T. Purvis. Mr. F. Purvis.	31	12	24	6	18	30	11	23	5	17	29
Mr. P. J. Athey. Mrs. Potts.	Apl 1	13	25	7	19	31	12	24	6	18	30
Mr. S. Armstrong. Miss Armstrong.	2	14	26	8	20	Jun 1	13	25	7	19	31

ANYONE NOT ABLE TO TAKE ROSTERED TURN MUST PROVIDE A SUBSTITUTE.

The firewatching roster for Percy Crescent and Cockburn Terrace, North Shields. Compulsory firewatching was introduced for civilians so that they could report damage caused to commercial and industrial premises by incendiary bombs at night. Every firewatcher was required to carry out forty-eight hours of service a month.

THE HOME GUARD

The formation of the Local Defence Volunteers was announced in May 1940 to assist the defence of the country against invasion. Its name was later changed to the Home Guard. The organisation recruited approximately 500,000 men between the ages of 17-65. Many of the men in their forties and older had seen service in the First World War and earlier wars. They were subject to the same military law as soldiers in the Army, and could be ordered to perform training and operational duty for periods not exceeding forty-eight hours in each period of four weeks.

Having fulfilled its role, the Home Guard ended its wartime service in December 1944.

In Co Durham there was a total of twenty-four Home Guard Battalions, and in Northumberland, eighteen.

Normally, a Home Guard Battalion would consist of over 1,000 men. Young men often spent a period in the Home Guard before being called up for full military service.

Members of 18th Durham (West Hartlepool) Battalion Home Guard marching through the town.

Officers of 2nd Durham (Chester-le-Street) Battalion Home Guard including back row: Sandy Gordon, Mr Leybourne (Lloyds Bank Manager), Leslie Norman (Building Contractor). Front Row: Major H. Dixon (Adjutant), Lieutenant Colonel Len Usher (Auctioneer), Dr Lloyd (Medical Officer). Colonel Usher had served with the Canadian Army in the First World War when he was severely wounded.

Members of No 1 Platoon, No 6 Company, 4th Northumberland (Hexham) Battalion Home Guard at Haydon Bridge, Northumberland.

Home Guard dispatch riders at Burt Terrace, Gateshead.

Motor Cycle dispatch riders of 18th Durham (West Hartlepool) Battalion, Home Guard in front of the town's War Memorial.

Home Guardsmen, probably from the 11th Durham (City of Durham) Battalion, outside Durham Castle.

Home Guardsmen of the Signals Section of 7th Northumberland (Tynemouth) Battalion.

Home Guardsmen, probably from 7th Northumberland (Tynemouth) Battalion, at Cullercoats. Cullercoats was the target of heavy enemy air attacks.

Home Guardsmen at Cullercoats.

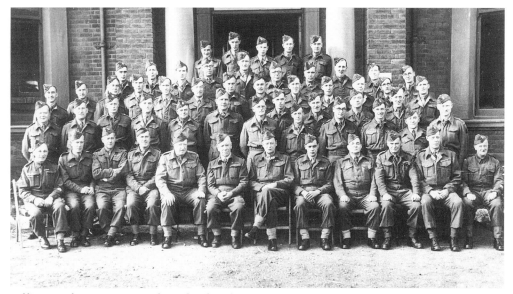

Officers of 109/101 Northumberland Home Guard Rocket Anti-Aircraft Battery. The use of the Home Guard and women of the ATS on operational duties in Anti-Aircraft Command enabled a saving of 71,000 regular gunners. Each night 178 Home Guardsmen were needed to keep an Anti-Aircraft Rocket Battery in action and as the rocket projectors had to be manned in eight shifts, about 1,400 Home Guardsmen were required for each rocket site.

Home Guardsmen of 2nd Durham (Chester-le-Street) Battalion at Pelton Fell, Co Durham.

Home Guardsmen of 15th Durham (Bishop Auckland) Battalion at
Spennymoor, Co Durham.

Home Guardsmen at Hall Field, Dinnington, Northumberland, 1944.

Home Guardsmen, probably from 11th Northumberland (West Newcastle) Battalion, at Westerhope, Newcastle, *circa* 1941.

Home Guardsmen, probably from 17th Durham (Barnard Castle) Battalion, on exercise at Wycliffe Hall, Whorlton, Co Durham, *circa* 1943.

Nurses and Home Guardsmen of the Ambulance Section of 20th Durham (Darlington) Battalion.

Home Guardsmen of 20th Durham (Darlington) Battalion at Stooperdale Shops, Darlington.

Home Guardsmen of 19th Durham (Stockton) Battalion.

Home Guardsmen of 'F' (Gray's) Company, 18th Durham (West Hartlepool) Battalion in 1944.

Members of staff from Richardson & Westgarth, Marine Engineers, West Hartlepool, who served in the Home Guard. This and other large businesses often had their own Companies of Home Guardsmen, which formed part of the local Home Guard Battalion.

Home Guardsmen of 16th Durham (Weardale) Battalion at Wolsingham, Co Durham.

A group of officers of 8th Battalion Durham (South Shields) Home Guard.

Home Guardsmen in the employment of R&W Hawthorn Leslie, Shipbuilders, Newcastle.

Officers of 'A' Company, 14th Durham (Houghton-le-Spring) Battalion, Home Guard, 3rd December 1944. Standing: 2/Lts P. Burns, S. Thorpe, S.H. Robinson, H. Lawson, J. Tubmen. Seated: Lt W. Northey MM, Capt E.A.B. Priddin, Major J.H. Brereton, Lt G.W. Siddel and Lt J.O. Dowell.

Home Guardsmen of 14th Durham (Houghton-le-Spring) Battalion parading in The Broadway, Houghton-le-Spring, Co Durham.

Home Guardsmen from Crook, Co Durham, with a crashed Messerschmidt 109 on display in aid of the Spitfire Fund, December 1940.

Home Guardsmen of No 4 Platoon, 'C' Company, 4th Northumberland (Hexham) Battalion at Newborough, Northumberland.

There were two battalions of Home Guard in Gateshead, 10th Battalion and 21st Battalion. Pictured are the officers of 21st Battalion. The Commanding Officer was Lt Col R.S. Sisterson.

Officers of the 22nd Durham (Wheatley Hill) Battalion, Home Guard.

Home Guardsmen of the 2nd Durham (Chester-le-Street) Battalion at West Pelton.

Home Guardsmen from Beamish, West Pelton and High Handenhold who were in the 2nd Durham (Chester-le-Street) Battalion.

March Past of Home Guardsmen, probably from 17th Northumberland (Ashington) Battalion, at High Pit, Cramlington, Northumberland, 1942.

Home Guardsmen, possibly from 16th Durham (Weardale) Battalion, at East Hedleyhope, Co Durham.

SECTION FOUR

THE CIVILIAN
UNIFORMED SERVICES

During the war, full-time police officers were assisted by part-time officers. Full time firemen were joined at night by part-time auxiliaries. Other organisations such as the Civil Defence, Royal Observer Corps, and the Women's Voluntary Service (WVS) also played major roles.

Members of the Auxiliary Fire Service in South Shields after the air raid on 2nd October 1941. (See page 24.)

Members of the AFS with a motorised water pump at Brandon, Co Durham, on 1st December 1939.

Members of the AFS at Nevilles Cross, Durham, on 1st August 1941.

Members of West Hartlepool Auxiliary Fire Service.

Mavis Pattison, who served with the AFS in Sunderland was the wife of Alan Pattison (see page 75). She is pictured with their daughter Adéle.

Members of the AFS from West Boldon, Co Durham, at 'The Dell', West Boldon.

Members of Auxiliary Fire Service, Newcastle, *circa* 1940.

ARP personnel of the Consett Iron Company, Co Durham.

A procession moving towards Durham Cathedral on 12th November 1939 of the Mayor, Councillor S. Kipling, and men and women who were manning ARP posts around the city.

Training of ARP nurses at Hetton-le-Hole, Co Durham, on 28th March 1941.

ARP Wardens at Sacriston, Co Durham. Notice the bells and rattles which were intended to give warnings of air raids. A stirrup pump can be seen in the foreground. These were used to put out minor fires.

Members of the Civil Defence at Thornley, Co Durham. The Civil Defence included wardens, rescue and stretcher parties, staff of control centres and messenger boys.

Members of the Royal Observer Corps at Millfield, Northumberland, *circa* 1941. Members of the ROC were largely unpaid volunteers. They worked in pairs and passed on information to the RAF about numbers, type, height and direction of aircraft believed to be hostile.

Dorothy Hall in the uniform of the Women's Auxiliary Police Corps, which she joined in November 1941. She was stationed in Co Durham, firstly at Whickham and then at Barnard Castle. Members of the WAPC carried out a variety of work including clerical duties, and as drivers and telephone operators.

PC Jim Middleton who was stationed at Amble, Northumberland. He is wearing the typical uniform of a wartime police officer.

A WVS Mobile Canteen at WVS Headquarters, Ashfield House, Joicey Road, Low Fell, Gateshead. Mrs Wilson is on the left and Mrs Godwin the right. The canteen was a gift from the American Red Cross.

SECTION FIVE

THE CIVILIAN WORKFORCE

During the war there was an inevitable demand for civilian workers in areas such as the production of food and munitions, coal mining, the building of aircraft and ships, the manufacture of vehicles, and the operation of public transport. This meant employment was available for every able and willing adult, and many young people of school leaving age. There were cases of very elderly men returning to their industries, and bringing with them their valuable skills and experience. Many people were effectively carrying out two jobs, continuing with their usual work and also serving in organisations like the Home Guard or ARP.

Women worked in factories, shipyards, agriculture and on buses, trams and railways. Several photographs in the book show them wearing trousers, which some people at the time found rather shocking. Many women, who had been widowed as a result of the war, had to go out and find work to keep themselves and their families, and they undertook training for teaching and other new careers.

The contribution of civilian workers, many of whom would have liked to have joined the armed forces had they had the choice, cannot be underestimated.

Tram staff, Sunderland, *circa* 1941.

Staff of the Royal Ordinance Factory, Aycliffe, Co Durham, who were
responsible for filling artillery shells.

A group of munition workers at ROF, Aycliffe.

Above: ROF Ammunition workers at Heighington, Co Durham.

Employees of Robert Sinclair Tobacco Company, Newcastle, ready for firewatching duty.

Workers checking 500 lb bombs after machining at the Davy Roll Company, Bedewell Works, Jarrow, Co Durham, 1943.

Women war workers employed by Whessoe, Darlington, with Mr T. Moore, foreman.

A Home Guardsman and a conductress stand in front of a Stockton Corporation Daimler Bus, Registration Number FPT 468. The destination board reads 'FAIRFIELD. Bishopton Road.' In addition to the Corporation's coat of arms, the bus bears some enlarged regimental badges. Note the white line along the bottom of the bus, which was to aid visibility when there were no lights in the streets because of the blackout, which was imposed nationally to make it difficult for enemy planes to navigate.

A group of Gateshead tram drivers and conductors during the Second World War.

Postwomen in Darlington, May 1941.

Above: Coal Miners at Sherburn Hill Colliery, Co Durham, 1940. Before the war there had been a great deal of unemployment among mine workers and there was still some unemployment during the early part of the war. However, by the end of March 1941 at least 16,000 miners in Durham had taken up other work since the outbreak of war and the demand for more coal added a great strain upon the industry.

Left: Raymond Basil Watkins at Craghead Colliery, Co Durham. He was called up to work as a Bevin Boy in 1944, earning £3 a week less income tax and paying thirty shillings for board at New Kyo Hostel. Bevin Boys were named after Ernest Bevin, the wartime Minister of Labour, were men aged between 18 and 25 who were chosen by ballot to work in coal mines instead of the armed forces.

AGRICULTURE

WHENEVER YOU CAN . . . .
LEND A HAND
ON
NEARBY FARMS

* Every hour counts!

The help of every countryman and countrywoman not already working on the land is urgently needed to make sure of this year's harvest. The nation's vital food depends on it. It takes 20 pairs of hands to deal with what one pair has sown. The men of the Forces who lent a hand last year are wanted for other tasks. It is up to you to take their place. Every hour counts.
The farm near your home can use all the time you can spare from other tasks. **Decide now when and how you can help.**

The Durham War Agricultural Executive Committee is organising what are known as LAND CLUBS, each of which has its own Secretary, whose members will go out in groups to any nearby farmer needing assistance. Already many clubs are in existence in many parts of the county, but to enable the scheme to function efficiently it is necessary there should be a club in every Town, Village and Hamlet in the County. As farms most likely to be in need of assistance are situated in more remote districts, CYCLING CLUBS should combine profit and pleasure by forming Land Clubs among their members. Those forming new clubs should notify :

THE LABOUR OFFICER, SCHOOL OF AGRICULTURE
HOUGHALL, DURHAM

Issued by the Ministry of Agriculture
for the Durham War Agricultural Executive Committee.

Left: A Ministry of Agriculture newspaper advert encouraging people to help on farms, July 1943.

The production of food was critical, particularly when little reliance could be placed on imports from other countries. Rationing of meat, sugar and butter was introduced early in 1940 and other food was added later. Like each other county, Co Durham and Northumberland had War Agricultural Executive Committees, which controlled agricultural work in the counties by giving orders as to how land was to be used, and dealing with farming considered to be inefficient.

A major role in farming during the war was played by the Women's Land Army. It was organised on a county basis, each with a County Chairman and County Secretary at the head. The types of work available included timber measuring, forestry, milk rounds, fruit growing, market gardening, glasshouse work, dairy farming, poultry farming, tractor driving, sheep farming, and general farming. There were even 'Girl Ratters', who were specially trained in destroying rats.

Members of the Women's Land Army stooking oats at Durham on 23rd August 1940.

A manual was written (by a man) for members of the Women's Land Army, and this gave a variety of information including the terms of employment. In 1941 the minimum weekly wage for a woman over 18, and the wage for working a week of up to 48 hours, was 32 shillings. The overtime rate was 8d an hour. If billeted in the farmhouse a woman had to receive a minimum of 16 shillings a week in addition to free board and lodging.

A uniform was provided, and this consisted of a serviceable rainproof mackintosh, khaki overall coat, two fawn shirts with turn down collars, pair of corduroy breeches, pair of dungarees, a green knitted pullover, three pairs of fawn stockings, pair of heavy brown shoes, pair of rubber gum boots, brown felt hat, green armlet with red royal crown, and a badge of the 'button-hold' type to wear in civilian clothes.

The manual also gave advice on how Land Army girls should conduct themselves. For example, a section on 'Make-up' related:

'Town girls on the whole use far more make-up than Country Girls. The Women's Land Army Volunteer should therefore be prepared to 'tone down' her lips, complexions and nails considerably.

The Volunteer will soon find that, as the other girls from the village do not use make-up, she will prefer not to use it herself, so as not to look conspicuous. She will find, too, that she will get such healthy glow to her cheeks that rouging will not be necessary!'

Land Army Girls ready for forestry work at Butterhaugh Nursery, Bellingham, Northumberland, *circa* 1943.

Land Army Girls at Stocksfield, Northumberland, *circa* 1942.

Land Army Girls who were billeted at the Land Army Hotel, Gray Road, Sunderland.

Land Army Girls at Consett, Co Durham.

Land Army Girls on a Fordson Tractor at the County School of Agriculture, Houghall, Durham, on 28th September 1939.

Women's Land Army girls loading hay at Bothal, Northumberland, *circa* 1940.

Agricultural workers preparing a pike of hay at Willimontswyke Castle, Bardon Mill, Northumberland, in 1941.

Publicity for the wartime 'Dig for Victory' campaign, Durham. Many people grew food for themselves in gardens and allotments and often kept poultry and pigs.

Staff of the Durham County War Agricultural Committee at the County School of Agriculture, Houghall, Durham, in September 1944.

THE ARMED FORCES

Many thousands of men and women from the two counties served in the forces. This book can only portray a very small percentage of them, and only a few of the units in which they served, but the selection is intended to give an indication of the diversity of service and provide some examples of deeds of bravery.

General, The Viscount Gort.
(Reproduced by kind permission of the Imperial War Museum.)

Lord Gort's family name was Vereker, and one of the Vereker family homes was Hamsterley Hall, Co Durham. This photograph was taken in 1940 when Lord Gort was Commander in Chief of the British Expeditionary Force. Historians consider that Gort's tactics made the Dunkirk evacuation possible, so saving many troops. In April 1941 he became Governor and Commander-in-Chief of Gibraltar, and then of Malta in 1942 where he is acknowledged to have led the island's defence with great distinction. He became a Field Marshal in 1943 and, in 1944, was appointed as High Commissioner and C-in-C Palestine.

A soldier of great bravery during the First World War, he had won the Victoria Cross, the Distinguished Service Order and two bars, and the Military Cross.

Lord Gort's brother, Lt Col the Hon S.R. Vereker MC, served as Commanding Officer of 5th Durham (Hamsterley) Battalion, Home Guard.

John Blight, RAFVR, of Chester-le-Street pictured extreme left in the back row, was a pilot in 224 Squadron, Coastal Command, based at St Eval, Cornwall, flying Lockheed Hudsons. He and all other members of his crew were lost on a mission over the French Coast on 6th February 1942.

Alan Pattison, RAFVR, was the middle of three brothers from Sunderland who were all Royal Air Force pilots. He served with 120 Squadron, and was killed in action in 1942. The youngest brother, Eric, was killed whilst flying in Canada in 1943.

The Prime Minister, Winston Churchill, and Mrs Churchill visiting the new General Headquarters Battle School at Barnard Castle, Co Durham, 1942.

David Souter of Gosforth, Newcastle, had joined the Royal Naval Volunteer Reserve in 1936 as a Midshipman. He served throughout the war in the RNVR, firstly in Motor Torpedo Boats and was the first member of the RNVR to be given command of an MTB. Operating from Gosport and Felixstowe his service included two and a half years in the Mediterranean, with eight months in Malta where he was appointed No 1 of the Coastal Force Base. Thereafter, he served in Destroyers off the East Coast of the UK, and escorted Troop Carriers for the invasion of France on D-Day.

David Souter on his MTB in the Mediterranean.

Dixon Scott of Gosforth was an officer in 2nd Battalion, Royal Northumberland Fusiliers, and saw service in North Africa and Italy.

Frank Glen of Pittington, Co Durham, who became a pilot in the RAF in 1941. He served in operations over Germany and then as a test pilot in India. He was awarded the Air Force Cross and was mentioned in dispatches.

Tom Wilson of Bishop Auckland, Co Durham, joined 4th Bn, Northamptonshire Regiment and was later with the Royal Military Police. He saw service in North Africa, the Middle East, Greece and Italy where he was wounded at Cassino.

Joe Kayll of Sunderland, a Spitfire Pilot, was awarded the DSO and DFC when he was commanding 615 Squadron, Royal Auxiliary Air Force in France in the spring of 1940. He led the squadron during the Battle of Britain in the summer of the same year. In June 1941 he was appointed to command the famous Hornchurch Wing. Towards the end of that month his engine was hit by enemy fire over France but he managed to bring the plane down safely in a field. He was taken prisoner by German troops and was eventually sent to Stalag Luft III in Silesia. There he organised escapes including the 'Wooden Horse' plan when three men escaped back to England. For his escape work he was awarded the OBE. He is seen here receiving both the DSO and DFC from the King in 1940.

This remarkable photograph was secretly taken by a brave French woman just after Joe Kayll had landed his damaged plane and been captured by German troops.

Robert Henderson, RAFVR, from Coxlodge, Newcastle, was a member of 221 Squadron. He was killed in April 1943 while serving in Malta.

John Henderson of Gosforth, Newcastle, served in 124th Field Regiment, Royal Artillery. He was killed in the Western Desert campaign in June 1942.

George Henderson (brother of John Henderson and cousin of Robert Henderson) of Gosforth, Newcastle, joined the Royal Navy in 1942 and served in the Mediterranean, the Middle East and the Far East. He is pictured front row centre in December 1942.

Right: Jack Long of Chester-le-Street volunteered for the Royal Navy and joined the Gunnery Branch. He was posted to DEMS (Defensively Equipped Merchant Ships Section) and lost his life as a result of enemy action while serving on a convoy in the English Channel in June 1944.

Below: The telegram received by Mrs Elizabeth Long on 29th June 1944 to say that her husband Jack (not John as incorrectly written down in the telegram) Long had been killed on war service. Their son, Ronald, then aged eleven, recalls returning home with his mother and grandmother from a shopping treat in Durham and picking up the telegram and handing it to his mother, not realising the fateful contents.

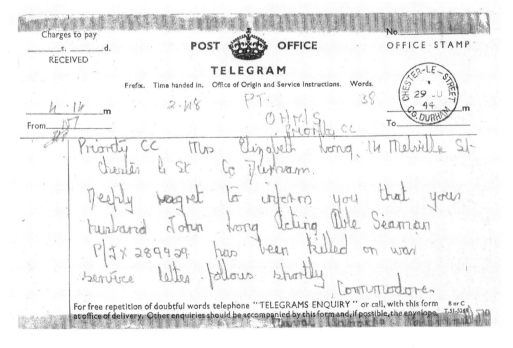

Tom Metcalfe MC of West Hartlepool was commissioned into 85th Heavy Anti-Aircraft Regiment, Royal Artillery, in 1939 and subsequently served in the North African and Italian campaigns. In North Africa he was commended for gallantry in rescuing an airman who had crashed in the sea and he was later awarded the MC for gallantry in action in Italy.

Jim Storey of Sunderland served in the Durham Light Infantry and the Royal Artillery. He was Officer Commanding a Battery in 47th Searchlight Regiment, which mainly consisted of men from the Sunderland area, and then in 112 LAA Regiment when 47th Searchlight Regiment was re-designated as a Light Anti-Aircraft Regiment. 112 LAA Regiment saw action in North West Europe.

Thomas Henry Graham from Lynemouth, Northumberland, served with 48th Light Anti-Aircraft Regiment, Royal Artillery, which sailed from Scotland to the Far East in December 1941. The regiment was captured by the Japanese in Java, and many of its members, including Thomas Henry Graham, were sent to Prisoner of War Camps in Japan.

The author's father, Alan Berriman of Fence Houses, Co Durham, in Algeria, August 1944. At the outbreak of war he was a Territorial Army Officer in 2/5th Battalion Durham Light Infantry (55th Searchlight Regiment). He served throughout the UK with Anti-Aircraft Command and then in North Africa and Italy, and was awarded the Czechoslovakian Medal of Military Merit First Class for his work with the Czechoslovakian forces.

George Ward, RAFVR, of Low Fell, Co Durham far right, was a Mid Upper Gunner in 582 Squadron, which formed part of the Pathfinder Force. He was awarded the Distinguished Flying Medal. His citation for the medal read: 'He has on a number of occasions shown great coolness and determination in driving off enemy attacks, and has at all times set and maintained a very high standard of operational efficiency.'

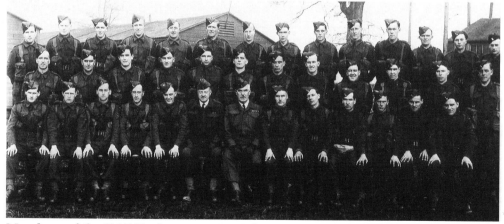

Members of the RAF Regiment on 1st February 1942, the first day of the formation of the Regiment. Jack Geddes of Witton Gilbert, Durham, who joined the RAF in 1940, is shown seventh from right, back row. He later served in the Far East. The RAF Regiment was established to protect airfields from the threat of attack by airborne troops.

Members of a Searchlight Cluster Site near Fallodon Hall, Embleton, Northumberland, August 1941.

Searchlights were used primarily to assist nightfighter pilots and anti-aircraft gunners by illuminating enemy aircraft. Overseas they were also employed to illuminate enemy ground forces by a method known as 'artificial moonlight', which involved reflecting the light from clouds on to the ground. A further use of searchlights was to direct aircraft back to safe landing grounds at night.

Cluster Sites were introduced late in 1940 when it was thought that a group of three searchlights would be more effective than having individual searchlights some distance away from each other, but the single site system was reverted to a year later.

Two Searchlight Regiments, Tyne Electrical Engineers (37th Searchlight Regiment) and 5th Battalion, RNF (53rd Searchlight Regiment) originated in Northumberland; and three, 47th (DLI) Anti-Aircraft Battalion, 1st/5th Battalion DLI (54th Searchlight Regiment) and 2nd/5th Battalion DLI (55th Searchlight Regiment) in Co Durham.

The men in the photograph are from 410 Battery of 53rd Searchlight Regiment, which firstly manned sites in Co Durham and Northumberland. In 1944 it was posted to the Isle of Wight where it was deployed against flying bombs also known as 'V1s', 'Doodlebugs', 'Divers', or 'Pilotless Aircraft'.

Peggy Hughes (née Trainer) of Pendower, Newcastle, pictured with her father in 1943. She was a member of 93rd Searchlight Regiment, Royal Artillery, a unique regiment in the British Army, which was composed almost wholly of women. The regiment was formed in 1942 and was deployed in and around North London. Unlike the men's Searchlight Regiments, the women in this regiment were not allowed to carry arms, nor could their searchlight sites be protected by anti-aircraft machine guns.

Driving pool of ATS members at the ROF, Aycliffe, Co Durham.

Members of the ATS clearing snow in front of Nevilles Cross College, Durham, in 1941.

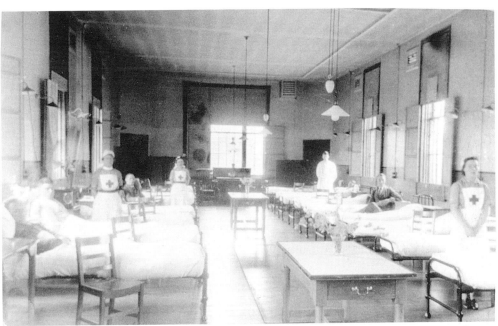

Fenham Barracks Hospital, Newcastle, after the evacuation of troops from Dunkirk in June 1940. Following the evacuation, wounded troops were sent to hospitals all over the country.

Arthur Rodgers of West Hartlepool, pictured right with a Danish friend in Aarhus, Denmark, at the end of the war. He joined the RAF in 1940 and was posted to North West Europe very shortly after D-Day. He was engaged in code and cipher 'Special Duties' and had the important role of passing to senior officers top secret intelligence from ULTRA, the British security classification used to denote the information produced by the decryption of enemy radio messages.

George Tindale from Fence Houses, Co Durham, was a well known amateur cricketer and footballer who served in the Royal Artillery. He is seen here back row right in a football team when serving in North West Europe.

The crew of MTB 691, 53rd Flotilla, RN. Sydney Rutherford of Witton Gilbert, Durham, middle row, third left. He joined the Royal Navy in April 1943. This MTB carried out patrols in Home Waters, and sorties off the Dutch, Belgium and French Coasts.

Members of the crew of HMS *Cornwall* on Christmas morning, 1940. Included in the photograph are, front row, far left: 'Robbie' Robson of Gateshead; far right: Anderson, who worked in an insurance office in Grey Street, Newcastle. Middle row, centre: Sub-Lieutenant Hamish Lawlan RNVR of South Shields; far right: Signalman James of Chester-le-Street. Back row, far right: Leading Seaman Kirby of Newcastle. In 1941 Hamish Lawlan left HMS *Cornwall* to join submarines.

Edward Coates of Sunderland joined the RAF and played the banjo in the celebrated RAF Band. He died on active service in June 1944.

Robert Johnson was a Sub-Lieutenant in the Tyne Division RNVR at the start of the War. He first served in the cruiser HMS *Manchester*, which was involved in the invasion and evacuation of Norway in 1940. In November 1940 his ship took part in the Battle of Spartivento in the Mediterranean when the Italian fleet was put to flight. He was on the cruiser HMS *Fiji* when it was sunk with great loss of life in May 1941 during the Battle of Crete. Between 1941 and 1943 he served in ships protecting Arctic convoys to North Russia and in 1944 he saw service supporting the Allied landings in the South of France. He was twice mentioned in despatches.

Dick Annand of South Shields won the Army's first Victoria Cross of the Second World War in May 1940. He was serving in Belgium as a Second Lieutenant with 2nd Battalion, DLI, when the German Army attempted to cross the River Dyle. His platoon had already beaten off a strong attack and he then led a counter-attack against one group. After ammunition ran out, he drove out the group with hand grenades. That evening, although wounded, he again used hand grenades to repel German troops. The next day the battalion was ordered to pull back from the river, but on learning that his batman had been severely wounded and left behind, Dick Annand returned to the original position and brought his batman back in a wheelbarrow before losing consciousness as a result of his own wounds.

Other winners of the Victoria Cross from Northumberland and Co Durham included:

Robert Henry Cain and James Joseph Bernard Jackman, both of the Royal Northumberland Fusiliers.

Dennis Donnini from Easington, Co Durham, was serving in the Royal Highland Fusiliers. He was the youngest person to be awarded the VC during the war, winning it at the age of 19. On 18th July 1945 his platoon was ordered to a German village. The platoon came under heavy fire from a house and Fusilier Donnini was wounded in the head. Despite his wound he and other survivors charged down the road and hurled hand grenades through a window of the house. Wounded a second time, he kept firing his Bren Gun until he was killed.

William Henry Kibby, who was born in Winlaton, Co Durham. Serving with the 2nd/48th Battalion Australian Military Forces he was posthumously awarded the VC for gallantry in Libya. In October 1942 he took charge of his platoon after the platoon commander was killed. He silenced an enemy machine gun, and directed fire of his men. Under heavy enemy fire he went out to repair the platoon's lines of communication on several occasions, and on 30th/31st October was killed in action.

Richard Breen Stannard, who was born in Blyth, Northumberland. Serving in the Royal Navy, he showed great gallantry in Norway in 1940, saving his ship and many lives during enemy action. He also held the DSO and the Norwegian War Cross.

Adam Wakenshaw of Newcastle.

Adam Wakenshaw of Newcastle was posthumously awarded the Victoria Cross for gallantry in Tunis in 1942. He was serving with 9th Battalion, DLI, and was the member of the crew of an anti-tank gun. The crew immobilised an enemy vehicle towing a gun, before another enemy gun killed, or wounded members of the crew including Adam Wakenshaw. He crawled back to his gun and although his left arm was blown off he loaded the gun and fired five more rounds damaging the enemy gun and setting its towing vehicle on fire. A direct hit on the ammunition then killed him. His valour prevented the enemy from using their light gun on a nearby Infantry Company, which was then able to withdraw in safety.

The anti-tank gun manned by Adam Wakenshaw. It can be seen in the Durham Light Infantry Museum, Durham.

James Joseph Bernard Jackman was a Captain in the 1st Battalion the Royal Northumberland Fusiliers. On 25th November 1941 the British assault on El Duda Ridge at Tobruk, Libya, was being slowed down by enemy fire from anti-tank guns. He led his Machine Gun Company to ease the situation on the right flank of the British tanks. He then went into action on the left flank. His coolness and complete disregard for danger inspired his own men and the British tank crews. He was killed in action the next day and was posthumously awarded the Victoria Cross.

Robert Henry Cain was a Major in the Royal Northumberland Fusiliers attached to the South Staffordshire Regiment which formed part of the 1st Airborne Division. In September 1944 at Arnhem in The Netherlands his Company was cut off from the Battalion and was closely engaged with the enemy. He encouraged his men to hold out, and they stopped the enemy attacks. Though he was suffering from a perforated eardrum and multiple wounds, he refused medical attention. He was awarded the Victoria Cross for his gallantry.

The Durham Light Infantry was Co Durham's County Regiment and its Battalions, as with the Battalions of The Royal Northumberland Fusiliers, served in many different campaigns.

The 1st Battalion, which was a regular battalion, had been stationed in China before the war. It was sent to the Middle East in 1940 where it took part in the defeat of the Italian Army. Within two weeks of the outbreak of war, the 2nd Battalion arrived in France as part of the British Expeditionary Force. It was followed by 6th, 8th and 9th Battalions in January 1940, and later by 10th and 11th Battalions. The DLI Battalions distinguished themselves in some very heavy fighting and there were many men killed, wounded, or taken as POWs. The 2nd Battalion returned to the UK less than 150 strong.

The 2nd Battalion re-formed, and in 1943 went to Burma, where it again distinguished itself as part of the 14th Army in the war against Japan.

In 1941, 6th, 8th and 9th Battalions, which formed 151 Brigade, went to the Middle East, and fought with the 8th Army. Later, men of these units saw action in Italy, and they landed in France on D-Day for the campaign in North West Europe. 10th and 11th Battalions also served in North West Europe.

16th Battalion saw action in the Italian Campaign, and also served in Greece. Units of 18th Battalion took part in the Salerno and Normandy landings.

The three DLI Searchlight Battalions, 1/5th, 2/5th, and 47th Anti-Aircraft Battalion, all became part of the Royal Artillery in July 1940.

Ian Turnbull of Chester-le-Street was a Captain in 8th Battalion DLI when he was killed on 2nd November 1942 during the second battle of El Alamein in Egypt. He is pictured with his mother, father and sister, Jean.

Soldiers of 6th Battalion DLI receiving Christmas Dinner in Egypt in 1942.

Bandmaster Frank Rose with the Band of 1st Battalion DLI at Brancepeth, Co Durham, in 1944.

Above: DLI Officers in a German Prisoner of War Camp, Oflag VIIc, in 1941. Six DLI Battalions had formed part of the British Expeditionary Force in France in 1939 and 1940. They returned considerably depleted after the German advance through Belgium in May/June 1940 and it is possible that these officers became POWs during that period.

Left: Lt Col William Watson was a solicitor from Barnard Castle, Co Durham. He commanded 6th Battalion Durham Light Infantry at the second battle of El Alamein, Egypt, in October and November 1942.

The Northumberland Hussars (nicknamed 'The Noodles') was a Territorial Army regiment associated with 15th/19th King's Royal Hussars, a regiment of regular soldiers which traditionally recruited in Northumberland and Durham. The Northumberland Hussars saw wide ranging service in Greece, Crete, the Western Desert, Sicily and North West Europe. Men of the Northumberland Hussars are shown here near Tel-El-Kebir, Egypt, in 1940. Back row, left to right: J. Lamb, W. Davidson, L. Murray, F. Robson. Front row, left to right: F. Chapman, R. Donald and N. Hale.

Soldiers of 'C' Battery 102 (Northumberland Hussars) Anti-Tank Regiment RA after the evacuation from Crete in 1942.

The King's brother, HRH The Duke of Gloucester, inspecting soldiers of 15th/19th King's Royal Hussars in Northamptonshire on 5th February 1941.

Arthur Fisher of Newcastle was serving with 274 (Northumberland Hussars) Light Anti-Aircraft Battery when he was killed in action on 22nd March 1943 at the Mareth Line, Tunisia, during the final battles in North Africa.

A welcome for soldiers from the Northumberland Hussars during the liberation of Brussels, Belgium, in 1944.

Soldiers of 15th/19th King's Royal Hussars drive through Eindhoven, The Netherlands, during its liberation in 1944.

Maurice Mather of Newcastle as a Troop Officer in 30th Searchlight Regiment somewhere in the South West on 3rd July 1941. This regiment, normally deployed in an Anti-Aircraft role, was at the time assisting the Civil Authorities in fighting devastating fires caused by enemy aircraft dropping incendiary bombs on the Bristol and Avonmouth Docks.

Les Bell of Little Black Hedley, Northumberland, served with the RAFVR. He is pictured centre in Antwerp, Belgium, in 1944 while attached to 72nd Polish Motor Transport Light Repair Unit. When the unit entered the southern half of the city, German forces were still occupying the northern half.

The King's sister, The Princess Royal, reviewing members of the ATS at Nevilles Cross College, Durham in 1941.

Soldiers of the 1/5th Battalion DLI (54th Searchlight Regiment) at Billingham, Co Durham in February 1940. The regiment initially recruited most of its men from the Stockton area. It was posted to North West Europe in November 1944 and played an active role in defending Brussels and Antwerp against German air attack.

The Royal Northumberland Fusiliers wore as part of its uniform the distinctive red and white hackle. Wherever its Battalions were in the world they celebrated St George's Day on 23rd April, when red and white roses were worn. Battalions of the Regiment served with the British Expeditionary Force, the Middle East, the Far East, Italy and North West Europe.

Some of the Battalions were re-deployed in non-infantry roles. The 6th Battalion was re-designated as part of the Royal Tank Regiment, and 5th Battalion, a Searchlight Battalion, became part of the Royal Artillery in July 1940. Units of the 4th Battalion served part of the war as Independent Machine Gun Companies.

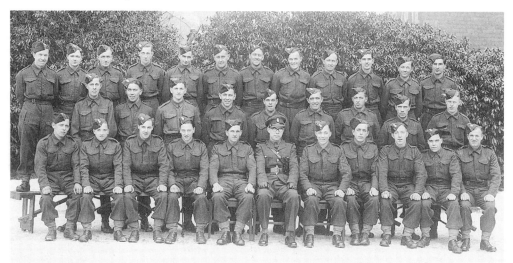

No 14 Platoon of Z Company, 9th Battalion, the Royal Northumberland Fusiliers.

43rd and 49th Battalions, the Royal Tank Regiment were formed from 6th Battalion, the Royal Northumberland Fusiliers. This photograph shows the officers of 49th Battalion. 43rd had a specialised role in experimental work and instructing other units. 49th went to France in August 1944 and was converted into an Armoured Personnel Carrier Regiment seeing action throughout North West Europe.

Soldiers of 4th Battalion, the Royal Northumberland Fusiliers, at Fontaine Bonnelieu, France, in May 1940. This Battalion was a Motor Cycle Reconnaissance Battalion and formed part of the British Expeditionary Force. It was later converted into Independent Machine Gun Companies and served in North Africa and North West Europe.

Soldiers of 1st Battalion, the Royal Northumberland Fusiliers, at Tobruk, Libya, in 1941. The 1st Battalion later seveRved in Italy.

The 9th Battalion, Royal Northumberland Fusiliers, was ordered to Singapore at the beginning of 1942 and after their ship was attacked by Japanese aircraft they disembarked on 5th February. By 12th February the situation was very grave for all British troops as the Japanese had complete superiority in the air. On 14th February Divisional HQ sent a message saying that agreement had been reached with the Japanese that firing should cease at 16:00 hours. This photograph taken by a Japanese officer shows the Battalion's Commanding Officer, Major Flower, who had gone forward under cover of a white flag to discuss the situation with the Japanese. Men of the Battalion, like other POWs in Japanese camps, endured appalling conditions, and 151 of them died. It has been recorded that 'throughout their long captivity the morale and bearing of all ranks of the Battalion remained at the highest standard.'

SECTION EIGHT

NORTHUMBERLAND AND DURHAM – A MISCELLANY

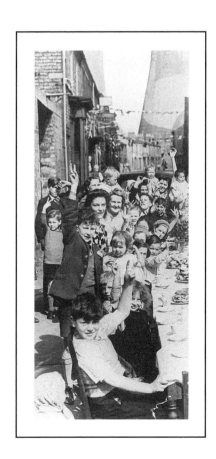

This Section features a variety of photographs of the lives and the work of Northumberland and Durham people during the war years.

Staff of the Gray Report Centre, West Hartlepool.

Civilians at West Hartlepool on 21st June 1940 reading a notice about air raid damage.

Girl Guides and Girl Cubs in Durham, July 1940. They had been collecting aluminium for the war effort.

Mayor of Durham, Councillor S. Kipling, receiving £6 10 shillings for the Ambulance Fund from Vera Tomlinson, Florence Hudson, Elizabeth Chapman, and Doreen Chicken on the steps of the Town Hall, October 1940.

A crowd in Durham Market Place awaiting the procession of Military and Civil Defence Services at the beginning of Durham, Brandon and Spennymoor War Weapons Week on 16th November 1940.

Miss Cecilia College, centre right, 'Queen of Ice' and World Champion Figure Skater at Durham Ice Rink on 19th March 1941. On the far left is the Mayor of Durham, Councillor J.F.J. Smith, who also owned the Ice Rink.

Boys and Girls in fancy dress at the Sacriston (Co Durham) Savings Group
Sports Demonstration, 19th September 1941.

Chester-le-Street Girls' Training Corps met at Bullion Lane School. The syllabus
for the GTC included First Aid, morse code, despatch carrying, physical training
and games, anti-gas instruction and a varied course of lectures on topics of
general interest. Mrs Edna Bowman is pictured on the right.

Evacuees from South Shields in the Lake District.

Another photograph taken in the Lake District of evacuees from South Shields.

Above: Children and staff of Barrington School, Stanhope, Co Durham, with sacks of foxglove leaves which were gathered widely during the war. The leaves were used as ingredients for medicines.

OFF THE ROAD —
but you can still get
RINGTONS TEA

BY instruction of the Ministry of Transport, the familiar Ringtons Vans have had to be taken off the road.

You can, however, still get Ringtons Tea, through specially-appointed distributing Agents.

Contact your Agent NOW, so as to ensure supplies of your favourite blend of Ringtons Tea in the new rationing period commencing July 25th. You will find the Quality and Flavour of Ringtons Tea still the best value obtainable.

Should you have any difficulty in obtaining supplies, send a post-card to the address below for name of your nearest Agent.

¶ The new selling plan applies to all Ringtons Products . . . Tea, Coffee, Coffee Essence, Cocoa and Baking Powder.

RINGTONS, LTD., Tea Merchants,
Head Office: Algernon Road, Newcastle-on-Tyne, 6.

Right: An advert for Ringtons Tea, July 1943. Adverts often contained references to wartime difficulties.

Advert for 'Salute The Soldier Week' at centres in
Co Durham, April 1944.

Above: The salute being taken from the Council Offices, Stanley, on 20th February 1942, during Warship Week when towns raised money to pay for the building of warships.

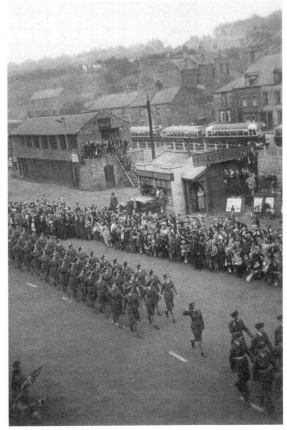

Right: A parade during War Weapons Week at South Burns, Chester-le-Street in 1941.

Harold Macmillan, far left, was the Member of Parliament for Stockton during the war. In 1943 he was appointed Resident Minister in North Africa. In 1944/45 he was attached to Field Marshal Alexander's Allied Forces Headquarters in Italy and became President of the Allied Control Commission in that country. He is seen here with Admiral Cunningham, the Prime Minister Winston Churchill and General Maitland-Wilson at Pomigliano Airfield, Naples, on 6th October 1944. Harold Macmillan was later to become British Prime Minister from 1957 to 1963.

(Photograph reproduced by kind permission of the Imperial War Museum.)

This photograph was taken on 14th July 1942 of Ship 529 which was being built at the yard of John Readhead & Sons on Tyneside. Shipyards on the Tyne, Wear and Tees, made an extremely important contribution to the country's war effort. Note the barrage baloons at the top of the photograph. These were tethered to the ground or to ships by wire cables and provided a defence against low flying aircraft.

Robert Cyril Thompson of East Boldon, Co Durham, was the Managing Director of the Sunderland Ship Builders, Joseph L. Thompson & Sons Ltd. He played a distinguished part in the wartime provision of shipping. In 1940 he went to the USA and Canada as Leader of the Admiralty Merchant Shipping Mission. In 1941 he was appointed Head of the British Merchant Shipping Mission, and in the same year was awarded the CBE at the early age of 34.

Soldiers of the Royal Army Service Corps with bus inspectors at Worswick Street Bus Station, Newcastle, during the Northern Bus Strike, which lasted from 10th until 23rd March 1945. The strike was over new schedules introduced by the Bus Company and the Army was called in to transport essential factory workers.

German Aircrew being escorted through the streets of Amble, Northumberland, by police and soldiers of the Royal Welch Fusiliers. The airmen had been picked up by a Fisheries Protection Vessel after their plane was shot down over Druridge Bay on 15th August 1940. They had flown from an airfield in Norway which was under German occupation.

German Prisoners of War at Featherstone Park POW Camp, Haltwhistle,
Northumberland.

A view of Featherstone Park POW Camp.

The interior of one of the huts at Harperley POW Camp, near Crook, Co Durham, which housed Italian and German POWs. The camp is now being restored and guided tours are available.

The chapel at Harperley POW Camp, decorated by the POWs for Christmas.

Armoured Cars in production at the Fabrications Shop, Caterpillar Works, Birtley, Co Durham.

Sections of Mosquito Aircraft manufactured at the Co-operative Wholesale Society Cabinet Factory at Pelaw, Gateshead.

Colonel Hereward Sprot of Wolsingham, Co Durham, in the uniform of the Local Defence Volunteers (better known as the Home Guard). He had formerly been a regular soldier and had commanded 3rd Dragoon Guards Carabiniers and 9th Battalion, DLI.

The author's uncle and aunt, Gordon and Betty Berriman, outside 58 Bewick Road, Gateshead, in October 1944. At the time, Gordon Berriman was Curate at St Cuthbert's Church, Bensham, Gateshead.

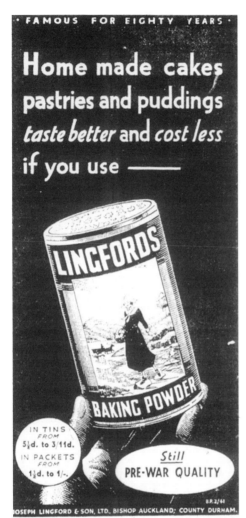

An advert for Lingford's Baking Powder, manufactured in Bishop Auckland, Co Durham.

Yes, they're both there alright . . . but the trouble these days is that biscuits aren't going into baskets often enough and in sufficient quantities!

We're sorry about this, but we're sure you don't begrudge the Services first call on supplies.

Even before the war Wright's Biscuits could never keep pace with the demand. Now that production is restricted we are doing our best to see that every stockist gets a fair share of deliveries.

Ask for Wright's DIGESTIVE, GINGER NUTS or DINNER WAFERS. **Quantity** is reduced but **quality** is as high as ever, and prices are as low as possible.

WRIGHT'S BISCUITS LTD. SOUTH SHIELDS

An advert for Wright's Biscuits, June 1941.

VE Day Celebrations in May 1945 at Angus Street, Langley Moor, Durham. At the end of the war, VE Day and VJ Day street parties were held all over the country.

Peace Celebrations Party at Lawson Street, Durham, in 1945.

Street Party at Stooperdale Avenue, Cockerton, Co Durham, in 1945.

Peace celebrations at Usworth Pit, Washington, Co Durham.

A street party at Brunswick Street, Darlington, 1945.

A VE Day
street party
in Wansbeck
Road,
Ashington.

A welcome home party at Linton Colliery, Northumberland, for men who served in the forces.

CITY & COUNTY OF NEWCASTLE upon TYNE

10

VICTORY CONCERT

CITY HALL, NORTHUMBERLAND ROAD,

ON THE DAY FOLLOWING VE DAY, 1945,

At 7 p.m.

ADMIT BEARER

(Doors open at 6·30 p.m.)

Please be in your
seat by 6·45 p.m.

Entrance by
Orchestra Door

A ticket for the Victory Concert at City Hall, Newcastle, May 1945.

THE PEOPLE'S HISTORY

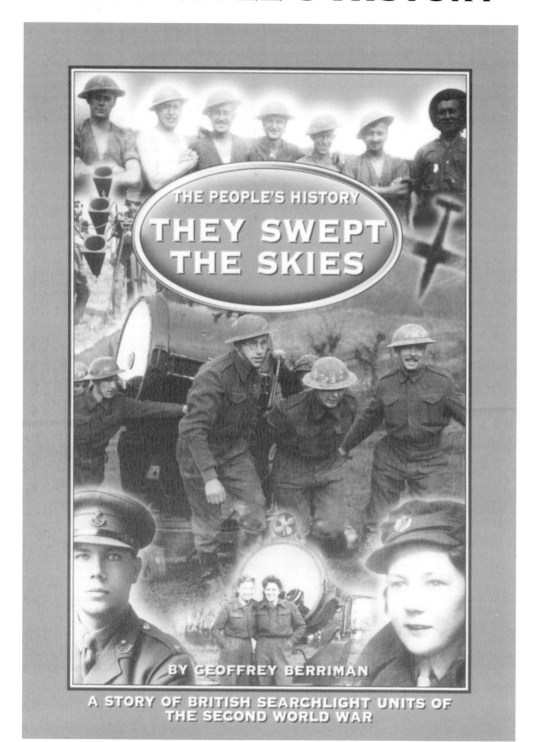

THE PEOPLE'S HISTORY

THEY SWEPT THE SKIES

BY GEOFFREY BERRIMAN

A STORY OF BRITISH SEARCHLIGHT UNITS OF THE SECOND WORLD WAR

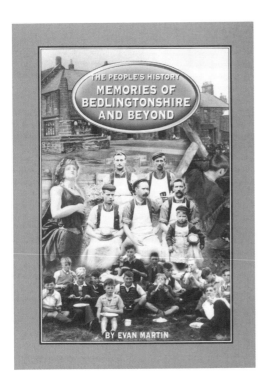

THE PEOPLE'S HISTORY
MEMORIES OF
BEDLINGTONSHIRE
AND BEYOND

BY EVAN MARTIN

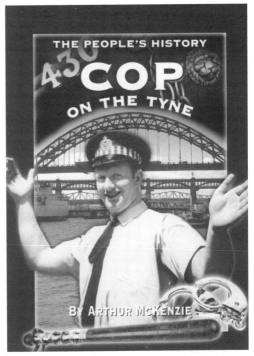

THE PEOPLE'S HISTORY
COP
ON THE TYNE

BY ARTHUR McKENZIE

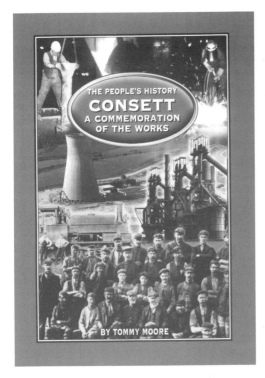

THE PEOPLE'S HISTORY
CONSETT
A COMMEMORATION
OF THE WORKS

BY TOMMY MOORE

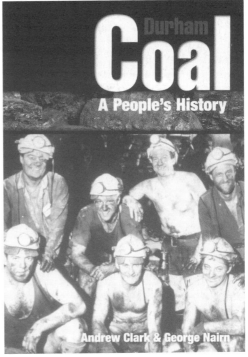

Durham
Coal
A People's History

Andrew Clark & George Nairn

Bibliography

I wish to acknowledge the following very helpful sources of information:

Ack-Ack by General Sir Frederick Pile. George G. Harrap & Co Ltd.

A Dictionary of The Second World War by Elizabeth-Anne Wheal, Stephen Pope, and James Taylor. Grafton Books.

The Durham Miners 1919-1960 by W.R. Garside. George Allen and Unwin.

Faithful – The Story of the Durham Light Infantry by S.G.P. Ward. Thomas Nelson Ltd.

The History of the Royal Northumberland Fusiliers During the Second World War by Brigadier C.N. Barclay. William Clowes & Sons Ltd.

Land Girl – A Manual for Volunteers in The Women's Land Army by W. E. Shewell-Cooper. English University Press.

Military Matters by Michael Tillotson – An article in *The Times*, 29th April 2005.

North East Diary 1939-45 by R. Ripley and B. Pears.

The Oxford Companion to the Second World War. General Editor: I.C.B. Dear. Consultant editor: M.R.D. Foot.

The Story of the Durham Light Infantry by Lieut. E.W. Short.

The Story of the Regiment – The Northumberland Hussars by Henry Tegner. Frank Graham.

Who's Who 1958 Edition.

The Author

Geoffrey Berriman lives in County Durham where he was born in 1949. He was educated at Uppingham School, and the University of Hull where he read Law. He has written several other books in the People's History series, including *They Swept the Skies* about British Searchlight Units of the Second World War.

The People's History

To receive a catalogue of our latest titles please send a
large stamped addressed envelope to:

The People's History Ltd
Suite 1
Byron House
Seaham Grange Business Park
Seaham
County Durham
SR7 0PY